T0401533

Panda Cubs

Julie Murray

Abdo Kids Junior
is an Imprint of Abdo Kids
abdobooks.com

Abdo
BABY ANIMALS
Kids

abdobooks.com

Published by Abdo Kids, a division of ABDO, P.O. Box 398166, Minneapolis, Minnesota 55439.
Copyright © 2019 by Abdo Consulting Group, Inc. International copyrights reserved in all countries.
No part of this book may be reproduced in any form without written permission from the publisher.
Abdo Kids Junior™ is a trademark and logo of Abdo Kids.

Printed in the United States of America, North Mankato, Minnesota.

102018

012019

THIS BOOK CONTAINS
RECYCLED MATERIALS

Photo Credits: Alamy, Getty Images, iStock, Minden Pictures, National Geographic Creative, Shutterstock,
©Quirky China News/Shutterstock p23

Production Contributors: Teddy Borth, Jennie Forsberg, Grace Hansen

Design Contributors: Christina Doffing, Candice Keimig, Dorothy Toth

Library of Congress Control Number: 2018945940

Publisher's Cataloging-in-Publication Data

Names: Murray, Julie, author.

Title: Panda cubs / by Julie Murray.

Description: Minneapolis, Minnesota : Abdo Kids, 2019 | Series: Baby animals set 2 |
    Includes glossary, index and online resources (page 24).

Identifiers: ISBN 9781532181665 (lib. bdg.) | ISBN 9781532182648 (ebook) |
    ISBN 9781532183133 (Read-to-me ebook)

Subjects: LCSH: Giant panda--Juvenile literature. | Baby animals--Juvenile literature. |
    Zoo animals--Infancy--Juvenile literature. | Bear cubs--Juvenile literature.

Classification: DDC 599.789--dc23

Table of Contents

Panda Cubs

Female pandas have 1 or 2 cubs at a time.

A cub is small. It is only
4 ounces (113 g) at birth.

It is pink in color.

9

It stays in a **den**. This keeps
it safe.

It drinks its mother's milk.

It grows fur. The fur is black and white.

14

The cub is 3 months old.

It comes out of the **den**.

It learns to walk and play.

16

It is 6 months old. It likes to eat **bamboo**.

The cub grows quickly.
At one year, it can weigh
100 pounds (45 kg)!

Watch a Panda Cub Grow!

newborn

12 months

18 months

4 years

Glossary

bamboo
a tropical grass that has hard, woody, hollow stems.

den
the resting place of some animals.

female
a girl animal that can have young.

Index

Abdo Kids ONLINE
FREE! ONLINE MULTIMEDIA RESOURCES

Visit **abdokids.com** and use this code to access crafts, games, videos, and more!

Abdo Kids Code:
BPK1665